DISCARD

IN THIS SERIES

THE COMPOSITE GUIDE

to **VOLLEYBALL**

RICHARD HUFF

BLACK MOUNTAIN MIDDLE SCHOOL
9353 Oviedo Street
San Diego, CA 92129-2198

CHELSEA HOUSE PUBLISHERS
Philadelphia

Produced by Choptank Syndicate, Inc.

Senior Editor: Norman L. Macht
Editor and Picture Researcher: Mary E. Hull
Design and Production: Lisa Hochstein
Cover Illustrator: Cliff Spohn

Project Editor: Jim McAvoy
Art Direction: Sara Davis
Cover Design: Keith Trego

First Printing

1 3 5 7 9 8 6 4 2

Library of Congress Cataloging-in-Publication Data

Huff, Richard M.
     The composite guide to volleyball / by Richard Huff.
          p.   cm.—
     Includes bibliographical references and index.
     Summary: Discusses the history of volleyball and the basics of the sport.
     ISBN 0-7910-5869-7
     1. Volleyball—Juvenile literature. [1. Volleyball.] I. Title: Volleyball. II. Title.
GV881015.34 .H84 2000
796.325—dc21
                                                           00-020117

29256

CONTENTS

1   LEADING THE WAY

Dr. Lazlo Kiraly had no intention of being in Atlanta on the night of July 28, 1996. Even though his son, volleyball legend Karch Kiraly, was ready to play for a record third Olympic gold medal in volleyball, the elder Kiraly planned to stay away. He was upset at the way the teams were selected for the 1996 Games, the first in which the sport of beach volleyball was officially sanctioned.

Dr. Kiraly had fled Budapest during the failed 1956 Hungarian revolt. He ended up in Santa Barbara, California, where he later would teach his son the game of volleyball.

But Lazlo, one of the sport's biggest boosters, known for waving the U.S. flag during the 1988 Olympics in Seoul, South Korea, and the 1984 Olympics in Los Angeles, had said he would skip the 1996 summer Games to protest a volleyball qualifying procedure.

His aversion to visiting Atlanta changed when Karch Kiraly and his beach volleyball partner, Kent Steffes, reached the finals, and his son called and asked him to be there.

"I've got a seat reserved for you on a flight to Atlanta in about four hours," Karch told his father on the eve of his Olympic finals performance. "Will you come?" Karch had spent most of the day arranging the plane tickets as well as tickets to the sold-out finals. His call convinced his father that he should be in Atlanta.

Karch Kiraly returns the ball against fellow Americans Mike Dodd and Mike Whitmarsh during their beach volleyball game at the centennial summer Olympic Games in Atlanta on July 28, 1996. Kiraly and his teammate, Kent Steffes, defeated Dodd and Whitmarsh for the gold medal.

Kent Steffes spikes the ball against his friend and opponent Mike Whitmarsh during their beach volleyball finals at the 1996 Olympics in Atlanta. That year marked the first time that beach volleyball was officially sanctioned as an Olympic sport.

Assured that his presence would not affect his son's play, Lazlo Kiraly packed his American flag and boarded a late-night flight to Atlanta.

It was the first year that beach volleyball, a two-man outdoor version of the classic indoor game, had been made part of the Olympics. The beach version, as the name suggests, is played on sand, which in many cases is trucked indoors for the contests. On the pro beach volleyball circuit, the games are played on beaches around the country.

The finals pitted Kiraly and Steffes against Mike Dodd and Mike Whitmarsh, fellow members of the American Volleyball Professionals (AVP), an organization that sanctions professional tournaments.

"It's nice to be in the position we're in," Kiraly told reporters before the final. "Even nicer still is that it's against two guys who I love to compete against and who are good friends."

For Kiraly, the Olympic finals completed a circle his father began when he started teaching his son the rules of the game.

Born on November 3, 1960, Karch started playing volleyball as a young boy, coached by his father. In high school his team won 83 straight matches and was undefeated in his senior year. He attended the University of California at Los Angeles (UCLA), where his efforts helped lead the team to a 124–5 record during his four years at the university.

In 1981 Kiraly was one of a handful of players invited to try out for the Olympic team. At the time the team was not very good and ranked 19th overall. Interest in the game was low and it wasn't easy to survive on the $10 a day the U.S. Volleyball Association gave the players. Occasionally, the payments amounted to just $100 a month. The players lived in an unfurnished apartment located in the flight path of the San Diego airport.

But Kiraly stuck it out. In 1984 he helped lead the U.S. team to a gold medal at the summer Olympics in Los Angeles, ending the Soviet Union's Olympic winning streak at three gold medals. There was some talk that the gold medal didn't count that much because the U.S.S.R. boycotted the 1984 Games. But the U.S. team responded by beating the Russians at the World Championships in 1985 and 1986.

The U.S. team then returned to the 1988 summer Olympics in Seoul, South Korea, to face the world, including the Russians. There, rather than being an also-ran, the U.S. men's volleyball team was the best.

"It's more of an accomplishment to win this tournament because of the better field," Kiraly told reporters then.

Kiraly then walked away from indoor volleyball and entered the professional volleyball arena. He was named the AVP's most valuable player in 1990, '92, '93, '94, and '95. On the pro circuit, he amassed more than 140 beach victories, more than any other player.

AVP tour member Mike Dodd drives the volleyball into the sand at the U.S. Olympic volleyball trials in Baltimore, Maryland. Dodd and his teammate, Mike Whitmarsh, made it to the Olympics but lost the gold medal to Kent Steffes and Karch Kiraly.

He returned to Olympic competition in 1996, when beach volleyball became part of the Games.

Now, almost a decade after his last Olympics, Kiraly found himself in the finals of the 1996 Games, heading for his third gold medal. Kiraly and Steffes defeated Dodd and Whitmarsh in the finals, 12–5 and 12–8.

"If I have to lose, I'd rather lose to the best, and Karch Kiraly has done more for volleyball than anyone else," Whitmarsh told reporters after losing in the finals.

"This was an awesome feeling," Kiraly said. "We put together an incredible tournament."

During Karch Kiraly's tenure at the top of the sport, interest in volleyball increased dramatically. In 1982, 15 million Americans played volleyball at least once a year. Today, more than 37 million players participate, with seven million playing more than 25 times a year.

"I personally feel obligated to be a role model," Kiraly said. "I take it willingly. We [AVP players] all work really hard to make our sport grow, so future players can have it better than we had it."

WHERE IT ALL BEGAN

2

William G. Morgan was born in the upstate New York town of Lockport in 1870. Morgan studied at the Springfield College of the Young Men's Christian Association (YMCA) in Massachusetts, where James A. Naismith, the creator of the game of basketball, had recruited him to play football.

After graduating from Springfield, Morgan worked at the Auburn, Maine, YMCA. In 1895 he moved to the Holyoke, Massachusetts, YMCA, where he took the job of director of physical education. In his new position Morgan was responsible for running the YMCA's sports unit and designing programs to suit the various age levels of the members.

The YMCA, founded in London in 1844, was created by young businessmen in response to growing concern over drinking and gambling among young men following the Industrial Revolution. The organization attempted to offset idleness through Bible studies and prayer meetings. The YMCA also emphasized the development of moral character and intellect through literary pursuits and sponsored lectures on a range of topics. By 1851, its success prompted its expansion to other industrialized countries. The first U.S. branch opened in Boston; by 1854, there were 26 YMCAs in the United States and Canada.

Young women enjoy a game of volleyball on the roof of the Brooklyn, New York, YWCA building sometime in the 1950s.

The first official game of volleyball was played at Springfield College on July 7, 1896, by this team. Standing at far left is William G. Morgan.

At the Holyoke YMCA, Morgan was well received. The number of participants in his classes grew, and he soon recognized the need for different sports that catered to his students' athletic abilities. Basketball, which James Naismith had introduced four years earlier, rapidly became popular. But Morgan believed the game was too strenuous and at times too physical for the YMCA's older members. The younger players didn't mind roughing it up from time to time, but Morgan needed an alternative for the association's more mature members.

Morgan invented a game he called "Mintonette," which blended portions of basketball, baseball, handball, and tennis.

The concept was simple: men on both sides of a 6' 6"-high net would hit an inflated ball across the center of the gym. Any number of players could be on either side and they could hit the ball as many times as necessary to return it to the other team. As Morgan refined the rules, the game was played on a court 25' wide and 50' long. The game lasted nine innings, with each team getting three serves before turning the ball over to the other side. If a serve was missed, players had a second chance. If the ball hit the net, it was considered a foul.

The object was to keep the ball going, which stands in stark contrast to today's version of the game, where the goal is to hit the ball to the ground so opposing players are unable to return the ball.

During a demonstration game of Morgan's "Mintonette," an observer noted that it appeared the players were volleying the ball over the net and that "Volley Ball" might be a more appropriate name. The game's inventor agreed, and the first official game of Volley Ball was played on July 7, 1896, at Springfield College. It was not until around 1950 that the name of the sport was lowercased and changed to one word, "volleyball," as we know it today.

After Morgan invented the game, it spread throughout the YMCA system. In the late 1890s, Morgan went to the Spaulding Manufacturing Company in Chicopee, Massachusetts, with specifications for a unique ball he had

The game of Mintonette, later called volleyball, was first played in 1896 at this YMCA building in Holyoke, Massachusetts.

designed for his game. Using Morgan's plans, Spaulding manufactured the first volleyball. In 1900, W. E. Day modified the rules for volleyball, which were then adopted by the YMCA. Under Day's rules, the net was elevated to 7' 6", and match length was set at 21 points.

Morgan, meanwhile, left his job at the YMCA and spent some time traveling. In 1910 he returned to his native town of Lockport, New York, where he and his wife raised five children. He took a job at the Harrison Radiator Plant, spending 19 years there before retiring. He died on December 28, 1942, a relative unknown. However, fans from around the globe reportedly visit his grave each year.

Thanks to members of the armed forces, the sport of volleyball became an international phenomenon. As soldiers were sent abroad to handle international skirmishes and wars, they also took along the game of volleyball, which they played away from the front lines.

According to the Volleyball Hall of Fame in Holyoke, Massachusetts, military officer Augusto York, who was part of the second military intervention in Cuba, introduced the game there in 1906. Two years later, a graduate student of Springfield College held a demonstration of volleyball at the YMCA in Tokyo. In 1910 the game was introduced in China and the Philippines.

Players in the Philippines created the style of play in which one participant hits the ball high so another can strike the ball hard at their opponents, which is believed to be the start of the set and spike style of play that is common today.

By 1914, volleyball was included in the recreation and education programs for all American soldiers. As a result, the game arrived in France and Africa during World War I. Dr. George J. Fisher, secretary of the YMCA War Work Office, made volleyball part of the training program at military camps. Thousands of balls and nets were sent to troops stationed around the globe.

Over time, the rules continued to change. By 1916, the score of an official game dropped from 21 points to 15; to win a match, a team had to win two out of three games. The net was lifted to 8'; and the ball weighed eight to 10 ounces. A player could hit the ball only once before another player hit it. That year volley-

Sailors enjoy a game of volleyball on the deck of a U.S. Coast Guard weather ship. Because it does not require a lot of space, volleyball has always been popular among sailors aboard Navy and Coast Guard vessels.

ball became part of the National Collegiate Athletic Association (NCAA), the body that oversees sports at colleges and universities in the United States.

The National YMCA physical education committee staged the first national U.S. tournament in Brooklyn, New York, in 1922. Six years later, the United States Volleyball Association (USVBA) was formed and recognized as the sport's governing body. The USVBA held the annual men's National Championships. The first USVBA woman's National Championships took place in 1949.

Just as volleyball was being introduced around the world, in southern California, some players were putting another spin on the sport. Rather than playing indoors, people were beginning to erect nets on the warm beaches. Volleyball record books show that the first two-man beach volleyball game was played in 1930 in Santa Monica, California, the widely acknowledged birthplace of beach volleyball. Soon, beach volleyball was played in such countries as France, Bulgaria, Czechoslovakia, and Latvia.

In 1947 the Federation Internationale de Volley Ball (FIVB) was organized in Paris with the USVBA as one of the charter members. By the late 20th century, membership in the FIVB grew to 210 member countries.

Just as the USVBA held championships in the United States, the FIVB initiated international volleyball championships for men in 1949 and women in 1952. The tournaments led to the acceptance of standardized rules and helped the sport gain admission to the 1964 Olympic Games held in Tokyo.

While indoor volleyball was taking off, beach volleyball continued to be primarily a California activity.

The sport was still a small draw. It usually took some sort of stunt to get people to come and watch, and more importantly, to take the sport seriously. The first official beach volleyball tournament held in 1947 was part of a beauty contest, which was staged to get people to watch the volleyball competition. Another beach tournament was held in Los Angeles in 1948, with the winners getting a case of Pepsi as their prize. By the 1950s, a series of tournaments took place on California beaches.

The men's and women's U.S. Olympic volleyball teams pose for their team portraits in 1964. Volleyball made its Olympic debut in 1964 at the Tokyo Games, where the Japanese women's team and the Soviet Union men's team claimed the gold medals.

The first beach volleyball association was formed in 1965, and in 1974 the first commercially sponsored beach volleyball tournament took place in San Diego. In the late 1970s, beach volleyball grew, with sponsors funding cash prizes for tournament winners. Interest in the beach version of the sport helped funnel more American players to the indoor sport. Some of the players who honed their skills on the California beaches became outstanding players for the indoor Olympic teams.

Indoor volleyball continued to draw the masses. In the early days, the sport was more popular abroad than it was in the United States.

The Soviet Union dominated indoor volleyball through the middle of the 20th century, winning more world and Olympic titles than any other country. The success of the Soviet Union was attributed to widespread entry-level interest and organized play and instruction at all levels. For example, 40,000 people turned out to watch the Soviet Union play in the 1952 World Championships in Moscow.

The Soviet Union won the first men's Olympic gold medal for volleyball in 1964, with Japan securing the women's gold medal. Four years later, the Soviet Union won both the men's and women's gold medals at the Mexico City Olympics. The Soviet Union's women's team repeated as gold medal winners at the Munich, Germany, Olympics in 1972, while the Soviet men's team finished with a bronze medal. The Soviet men's and women's team each finished with silver medals at the 1976 Olympics in Montreal, Canada. At the 1980 games in Moscow, the Soviet teams again took the gold medals.

The fate of the United States teams started to turn at the 1984 Olympics in Los Angeles. The Games were boycotted by the Soviet Union, in retaliation for the United States boycotting the 1980 Games in Moscow. With the Soviets out of the mix, the U.S. women's team took the silver medal, while the men's team earned its first Olympic gold medal.

Meanwhile, between the 1980 and 1984 Olympics, a full-fledged professional beach volleyball circuit was created under the leadership of the Association of Volleyball

Professionals [AVP]. By 1984 the AVP tour stopped in seven states, including New York, Arizona, and Hawaii.

The 1988 Olympics in Seoul, South Korea, marked the first time a resurgent U.S. team faced the Soviet Union in a full-fledged Olympic competition. The Soviet Union's women's team earned the gold medal, with the U.S. women finishing seventh overall. But in the men's competition, a U.S. team led by such players as Karch Kiraly, Steve Timmons, Dave Saunders, Doug Partie, Jon Root, and Craig Buck led the United States to its second consecutive gold medal.

Over time, the dominant U.S. team started to erode. In 1992 the U.S. men's and women's teams earned bronze medals at the summer Olympics in Barcelona, Spain. At the Atlanta games in 1996, the men's and women's indoor teams were shut out of winning medals.

Many of the top indoor volleyball players who had led the United States to earlier Olympic medals moved into the beach ranks, where they earned decent livings playing the sport they loved. For example, in 1995 the AVP Tour consisted of 29 events with more than $4 million in total prize money available for participants.

The inclusion of beach volleyball in the 1996 Olympic Games in Atlanta helped bring back some of the best players to Olympic competition, including Karch Kiraly and his longtime beach volleyball partner Kent Steffes.

Through the mid-1980s and into the late '90s, the play of folks such as Kiraly, Timmons, and Steffes helped bring the sport to more people than ever. It is estimated that more than 46 million Americans play volleyball in either formal games or backyard events. More than 800 million players around the world play at least once a week.

By 2000, the beach version of volleyball received the most attention on television, while indoor volleyball was ignored.

"Any beach is more attractive than the inside of [a] stadium. . . ." Kiraly told the *Chicago Tribune.* "You have natural sunlight, girls in bikinis, guys in shorts. What better way to make a living than going to the beach?"

3   THE BASICS

While more than 100 years have passed since William G. Morgan created the game of volleyball as a form of exercise for older men, the basic rules of the sport haven't changed all that much.

THE SETTING

A volleyball court is 29.5' wide by 59' long. The court is divided equally, with the sides being separated by a net 32.8' long and 3.3' wide, usually made from a thin mesh, with squares nearly four inches wide. Two posts on the sides of the court hold the net in place, with the top of the net set at 7', $11^5/8$" high for men, and slightly lower, 7', 4", for women.

Poles holding the net are equipped with antennae that extend up beyond the height of the net, creating a foul line-like marker. Players must keep the ball within those lines, but there are no limitations on how high the ball can be hit.

THE BALL

Though Morgan's YMCA students used whatever balls were available to play the game, today sports companies make a ball specifically for the sport. A volleyball has a leather cover without laces and is 25 to 27" in circumference. A volleyball weighs nine to 10 ounces, which

Holly McPeak digs against the Brazilian team of Jackie Silva Cruz and Sandra Pires Tavares during a match. Unlike indoor volleyball, beach volleyball is typically a two-on-two game.

makes it slightly smaller and lighter than a basketball.

THE RULES

Indoor volleyball teams consist of six people. Three players position themselves in the front of the court, near the net, and there are three back-row players.

The server—the team member who starts the volley—stands behind the court's back line and attempts to hit the ball over the net to opposing players. A typical serve involves a player tossing the ball overhead and then slamming it with the hand or fist. Some players also use an underhand serve, where the ball is dropped, and hit with an upswing. Servers get one attempt to hit the ball over the net.

Once the ball is successfully hit over the net, the object of the game is to hit the ball back and forth using heads, forearms, hands, or any other part of the body, to keep the ball aloft. The game continues until one team allows the ball to drop to the floor.

Teams must get the ball back to the opposing side within three hits. Once a player hits the ball, he or she can't touch it again until it's been hit by another team member or their opponent.

Only the team that is serving can score a point. For instance, if team A is serving, they score if team B drops the ball. If team A is serving and team A drops the ball, it does not count for team B; the serve then moves to team B.

A player serving the ball continues to do so as long as his or her team is scoring points. When the serve reverts to the opponent, the team rotates positions, one spot clockwise. For example, when rotating, the player occupying the right corner of the front row moves to the right corner of the back row. The player who was standing in the right corner of the back row moves left or to the middle of the back row.

Officials include a referee, scorer, umpire, and line judges.

The rules for beach volleyball are not dramatically different from those of the indoor game, though there are some variations. Typically, beach games are two-on-two. In

Mickisha Hurley, of the U.S., left, spikes the ball while her opponent, Nuris Arias of the Dominican Republic, tries to block. In volleyball, players spike the ball in hopes of slamming it just over the net, where it will hit the floor before an opponent can reach it.

Women's volleyball teams compete at an international contest held in Prague, Czechoslovakia, in the 1960s.

place of rotating, the players simply alternate serving.

The beach game requires less equipment. Male players usually wear shorts and a T-shirt or simply shorts. Women players often wear bikini-like sportswear. Most players wear hats or visors, gobs of sunscreen, and sunglasses to help with their vision. On the beach, players go barefoot.

The balls used for the outdoor game are less inflated and a little larger than indoor balls, which allows easier handling for outdoor events that can be affected by blowing winds.

A beach volleyball net does not have the same antennae as the indoor setup, with the exception being on the professional level. The height of the top of the net is also elevated to an even 8'.

Despite the differences in playing surfaces and the number of players on the court, the basics of both versions of Morgan's volleyball are the same. The ultimate goal is to slam the ball over the net and to the ground on the opposing team's side of the court, thereby preventing any chance for a return volley. Doing so requires players to execute a series of moves, such as a set, whereby a player hits the ball up so that a teammate can spike it down on the other side of the net. But getting to the point of a lightning-fast spike occasionally takes some passing between teammates. Another way to score or stop an opponent's serving is to simply block the ball as it comes over the net, causing it to drop to the floor.

In both the indoor and beach versions, the first team to score 15 points—and to do so with a margin of victory of two points or more—is declared the winner. In indoor volleyball the contest is built around a best-of-three match. Beach volleyball is based on a single-game competition.

On the AVP tour, a game is limited to nine minutes, eight for live television events. The clock runs when the ball is in play. Once time runs out, the team that is ahead by two points or more wins. If neither team is ahead by two points, play continues until one team has created a two-point margin.

4 VOLLEYBALL CATCHES ON

Though volleyball was created in the United States, it flourished in many other countries before truly catching on in the United States. Thanks in part to the soldiers who played the game abroad during World War I and World War II, the game took off in countries like Japan and the former Soviet Union, as well as all of Europe, where the sport was made part of physical education programs and national sports teams.

The sport gained a wide following in the Soviet Union because potential players were provided well-organized instruction at a variety of levels.

One of the best examples of a country and its people getting behind the sport of volleyball came from the Japanese women's Olympic team of 1964. The team generated extensive media interest because all the members of the team worked for the same company. Encouraged by the Japanese Volleyball Association, they devoted all of their free time and energy to training, practice, and competition under strict, but very talented, coaches.

With that sort of support on a variety of private and public levels, the Japanese women's volleyball team went on to be one of the most dominant groups of the mid-1900s. They earned the first Olympic gold medals for women's volleyball, and they won the World Championships in 1962, '66, and '67.

Players practice before the 1999 U.S. Olympic Cup beach volleyball tournament held in San Diego, California. In volleyball, the first team to score 15 points, provided they have at least a two-point lead, is declared the winner.

Harry E. Wilson, coach of the 1964 men's Olympic team, was one of volleyball's biggest promoters in the United States. The founder of the National Volleyball Review, *Wilson also led his YMCA team to 12 national titles between 1948 and 1964.*

Czechoslovakia, Hungary, Poland, Bulgaria, Romania, and the Soviet Union dominated the European Championships. In Asia, China, Japan, and Korea have won most of the titles.

In the United States, one of the early pioneers of volleyball was Harry E. Wilson, who was known as "Mr. Volleyball USA" for his work in pushing the sport. Wilson, who died in 1973, was the founding editor of the *National Volleyball Review*, which in 1947 was renamed and expanded to become the *International Volleyball Review.*

In addition to his publishing endeavors, Wilson served as president, vice president, and board member of the U.S. Volleyball Association, the organization that oversees the sport in the United States. Between 1948 and 1964, Wilson led the Hollywood YMCA volleyball team to 12 national titles. He coached the 1956 men's World Championship squad and the 1964 men's Olympic team, which finished ninth out of 10 teams that played in the first-ever Olympic competition for the sport. Wilson's contributions to the sport were considered so great the USVBA named an annual award in his honor to recognize a person's outstanding service to the sport.

On the beach volleyball front, Bernard Holtzman and Eugene Selznick were the men behind the growth of the sport in its early days. Holtzman was an all-American player and a member of the Hollywood Stars in 1948 when the team won its first National Championship. Between 1948 and 1974, the Stars won 14 YMCA national titles and a dozen American Volleyball Association titles. Holtzman organized the first official two-man beach volleyball tournament in 1947. He and Selznick were key factors in getting the beach version of the sport recognized as a real event, rather than as a sideshow to a beauty contest.

Although he didn't surface in the sport until more than 60 years after the beginning of volleyball, Pete Velasco was another pioneer worthy of Hall of Fame entry.

Velasco, who was born and raised in Hawaii, was the captain of the first U.S. Olympic team in 1964 and a member of the 1968 team in the Mexico Olympics. He was named the USVBA All-Time Great Player in 1970 and was made a first-team all-American 10 times between 1962 and 1972. Velasco was the first volleyball player elected to the Hawaii Sports Hall of Fame and Museum and was named to the National Association of Inter-collegiate Athletics Hall of Fame in 1980.

While the sport was growing around the world in leaps and bounds, it wasn't until 1970 that the NCAA created a men's volleyball championship. The first tournament was held at UCLA, whose team also won the first three NCAA titles. As an example of the West Coast's overwhelming competitive stronghold on the sport on a college level: a West Coast university has won every NCAA national championship. Only once since 1970 has an eastern school made it to the finals: in 1995, when Penn State lost to UCLA in the championship match.

Volleyball got its greatest boost in the United States in the early 1980s when a group of men under the tutelage of coach Douglas Beal took on the world. At that time, the U.S. men's indoor volleyball team was ranked well behind

Volleyball Hall of Fame member Pedro "Pete" Velasco, captain of the first U.S. Olympic Volley-ball team at the 1964 Olympics, was a first-team all-American for 10 consecutive years.

the dominant teams and had very little support from private and public corporations. There were no television contracts to support the team, which further hurt volleyball's chances of generating interest outside of its small pocket of followers.

But the Americans persevered and attempted to rejuvenate the sport by creating an Olympic team for the 1984 summer Games.

In early 1981 Karch Kiraly and Steve Timmons were among those invited to try out for the U.S. volleyball team.

Volleyball hadn't become a national phenomenon in the United States like it had in many European countries, where the sport trails only soccer in terms of popularity. The USVBA chose to focus on the National teams, rather then attempt to start nationwide coaching programs that could help grow the sport on a local level. By creating a supergroup of national men's and women's teams, the USVBA could generate nationwide interest in volleyball through their play.

To that end, Timmons and Kiraly, as well as such players as Chris Marlowe, Craig Buck, Dave Saunders, Marc Waldie, Steve Salmons, Dusty Dvorack, Pat Powers, Aldis Berzins, and Rich Duwelius, remained dedicated to the sport. Often living together in a small apartment and housing their possessions in their run-down cars, the team stuck together and gelled. For years they practiced four hours a day, between their jobs and training.

"We'd get right up and go straight to the beach for practice," Kiraly said. "Afterward, we'd leave our wringing, dirty clothes on and jump in the ocean. Then, we'd leave them

drying on the beach. That was our laundry break. Then, we'd play all afternoon."

On the women's side, Flo Hyman, Rita Crockett, Kim Ruddins, Julie Vollertsen, Paula Weishoff, Jeanne Beauprey, Debbie Green, and Rose Magers undertook a training program that asked more of the players than any other in the history of the sport. Like the men, the women's team members made extreme sacrifices for the opportunity to represent the United States.

Until 1984, the sport hadn't really captured the hearts of American fans. It was popular in high school gymnasiums and in select pockets of the country, but there was no

U.S. volleyball player Doug Partie, left, talks to team captain Steve Timmons during a match at the 1992 summer Olympics in Barcelona, Spain. The entire U.S. volleyball team shaved their heads to protest the overturning of their victory over Japan.

national rooting going on like there was for women's gymnastics or figure skating.

But the Olympic squad started a wave of interest in volleyball. Reportedly, Los Angeles souvenir salespeople couldn't successfully sell Olympic torch T-shirts, though once they added a volleyball image on the back, the shirts were sold-out. Scalpers asked as much as $500 per ticket to the Long Beach Arena, where the volleyball competition was held.

The fans' expectations of the American team's performance may have been higher than those of the players themselves. Prior to 1984, the best the American men had done in an Olympic competition was seventh. But in 1984 the men's team won the nation's first Olympic gold medal in volleyball. Overnight, interest in the sport soared.

"Our goal was to win a bronze, silver or a gold, any medal, at the '84 Olympics," Kiraly told the *Dallas Morning News*. "Then when we won the gold, things changed overnight. There was a demand for us to stay together. We had been planning to all go our separate ways. But the new demands made it so some of us could make a living at the game, rather than barely make ends meet, as we did from '81 to '84. We were able to put some money away, afford to buy homes, and make a much better living."

And stay together they did. The team also earned the gold medal at the 1988 Olympics. Their gold medal performances helped lure more fans and more corporate funding to volleyball, which ultimately helped lead to more players.

By 1989, the number of USVBA registered tournament players more than doubled to

46,258, up from 22,000 in 1984. That year, an exhibition game between the U.S. team and Cuba held in Minneapolis drew 14,789 people, then the team's largest audience ever.

The influx of corporate funding helped the USVBA increase its subsistence payments to team members from $10 a day when Kiraly started out to $700 a month for new players and as much as $20,000 a year for seasoned players. Others earned even more. Kiraly, for example, received an average of $70,000 in 1989. By 1995, he was earning $392,610 playing in the AVP Beach Volleyball Tour.

Growth notwithstanding, the sport still clearly lags behind others in the U.S. and other countries. When the International Volleyball Federation (FIVB) had a 100th anniversary of volleyball celebration, it staged a "100 Years of Volleyball in 100 Days" campaign in which there were tournaments in 100 countries, with the United States not among them.

Today, despite the performance of the 1980s Olympic teams and even the 1996 beach team led by Kiraly, the sport is still essentially known as something played in high school gyms and in backyards. Volleyball doesn't have the big-buck cache to make it a programming option for television. And without television, few think about the sport.

"In many parts of this country, there is still a stigma about volleyball, that it is a sissy

U.S. Olympic volleyball champion Paula Weishoff poses with her silver and bronze medals, which she won at the 1992 and 1988 Olympics.

game, the one to go out for if you can't win a [varsity] letter in anything else," Kiraly told the *Chicago Tribune* in 1995. "People don't realize what a difference there is between the picnic game and the top level."

The 1984 Olympic gold medal had a greater impact on beach volleyball than on the indoor version, where numerous efforts have been made to generate professional leagues. Even there, though, the growth has been problematic. Each of the major men's and women's indoor volleyball professional leagues have run into financial problems, in part because they've had trouble generating the kind of corporate sponsorships and broadcast contracts that are necessary to compete with major sports such as baseball, football, and auto racing.

"Before 1984, volleyball followed the original strategy of the YMCA, that it was a sport to be played for nothing more than enjoyment of the players and exercise," Reuben Acosta, president of the FIVB, told the *Chicago Tribune* in 1995. "[Then] we decided to go to a sport for spectators."

So far, efforts to boost volleyball's popularity have generated little in the way of increased awareness for the sport outside of the West Coast. Other than a few beach volleyball games shown on the sports cable channel ESPN, there is not much national exposure for the sport. The United States remains the only FIVB member without a men's professional indoor league.

"This country has a different set of priorities," Kiraly said. "It's the same thing with soccer as with volleyball. If soccer is going to struggle to have a pro league after the most successful [men's] World Cup in history, it's even more of a struggle for other sports."

According to USVBA statistics, there are nearly 40 million volleyball players in the country, with slightly more men than women playing.

"The United States is still living in the YMCA era," Acosta said. "This bothers me very much. The most powerful country left aside."

WOMEN MAKE THEIR MARK

Growing up in Long Beach, California, Flora Hyman read that the 1984 Olympics would be held in the United States. Then a ninth grade student, Hyman, a gangly teenager, set out to find a sport where she could excel and perhaps make an Olympic team to compete in Los Angeles. She selected volleyball and "charted my course from there," she told a reporter in 1984.

Best known as Flo, Flora Hyman found a home on the volleyball court at Inglewood, California's, Morningside High School. Always on the tall side, Hyman grew to 6'5" and developed into an exceptional hitter, able to spike the ball at an amazing speed.

Hyman, born in 1954, began playing volleyball on the college level while attending the University of Houston from 1974 through 1977. Because of her size, her speed, and her intense athletic ability, Hyman stood out on the court. She trained hard and put her heart into the sport, often at the expense of a normal life.

"When it all works well it feels like heaven," she said once. "You feel like you're playing a song."

If she were a singer, she would have been on top of the charts. As part of the National team, Hyman was set to play on the 1980 Olympic team. But as mentioned earlier, the United States boycotted the 1980 Games in Moscow, dashing the hopes of thousands of American athletes who spent most of their lives training for a shot at an Olympic gold medal.

Nancy Reno of San Diego, California, slams the ball as Germany's Danja Musch defends the net during their Olympic beach volleyball match at the 1996 Games in Atlanta, Georgia.

At 6' 5", Flo Hyman was one of the most imposing forces on the court, and she used her popularity as a volleyball player to promote greater opportunities for women in sports.

Rather than give up, Hyman stuck to her high school vow to make it to the 1984 Olympics, where she could play before a hometown crowd. Along the way, she continued to hone her skills and elevate her game.

"The audience would hold its breath when she rose for a spike," writer Joan Ackermann-Blount told *Sports Illustrated.*

It wasn't easy, though. The path to the 1984 Olympics went through a demanding coach named Dr. Arie Selinger, who had a reputation as a tough taskmaster.

He had been the coach of the National team since 1975 and was known as a disciplinarian. Early in their relationship, Selinger scolded Hyman for not pushing herself and not progressing as a player. Over time the coach forced her to reevaluate her play and to push her tolerance for pain.

Selinger pushed Hyman hard. He urged her to be more aggressive and to dive after a ball headed for the floor.

"I had to learn to be honest with myself," she said. "I had to recognize my pain threshold. When I hit the floor, I have to realize it's not as if I broke a bone. Pushing yourself over the barrier is a habit. I know I can do it and try something else crazy. If you want to win the war, you've got to pay the price."

Hyman was named the best hitter of the 1981 World Cup Games and was selected to the All-World Cup Team, a group of the world's best volleyball players.

She became a captain of the team and a moral leader to her teammates.

"I used to sit up late at night and just listen to her," former teammate Dieter Collins told the *New York Times.* "You'd see Flo play and you'd want to be just like her."

Hyman led a confident U.S. team into the 1984 Olympics. But the Soviet Union refused to attend the 1984 Games in Los Angeles, so the volleyball contest was without one of its key challengers. The absence of Russia didn't diminish the competition level at all, though.

The U.S. team worked its way into the championship match against the powerful Chinese team.

"We've been working [for the gold] ever since we decided to pursue being on the national team," Hyman said before playing China. "The gold medal to us represents spirit."

At age 30, Hyman realized she was probably going to be playing in her first and last Olympics.

"My commitment to myself was 1984 because 1984 meant the games would be at home," she said then. "I knew it would be a good way to go out."

Earlier in the competition, the U.S. women's team had beaten China. But in the championship match, China rebounded to beat the U.S. women's team, which earned the silver medal in defeat.

But by the end of the 1984 Olympics, Hyman was considered the best volleyball player in the world.

Hyman then announced that she would retire. Asked what she'd do next, she didn't have an answer.

"I'm officially retired," she said. "But I'm going to stay for the first year [of retirement] in the program and help the young players.

I'd like to ease their way. After that, I don't know."

Hyman's retirement didn't last long. After the Olympics, she left to join a club team in the Japanese national league. There, on January 24, 1986, after being called to the bench during a game, Hyman fell dead of a ruptured aorta caused by Marfan's syndrome. Her death rocked the volleyball world.

"She was older than me and kind of kept me in line," teammate Rita Crockett told the Associated Press in 1998. "She was like my mother, like my sister. When I saw her lying on the floor, I just ran off the court to see what

Lisa Arce lunges for the ball during the Oldsmobile Alero Beach Volleyball Championship match. Together with teammate Barbara Fontana, Arce defeated Annette Buckner Davis and Jenny Johnson Jordan, 15–12.

happened. They said she would be okay, that she just fainted, because they didn't know."

Crockett continued to play but soon asked to leave. By the time Crockett got to the hospital, Hyman was dead. She was 31 years old.

Though her life was cut short, Hyman was an influential figure in women's sports. She pushed for opportunities for women athletes and lobbied for the Civil Rights Restoration Act, which was designed to guard against gender discrimination in high schools and colleges.

Since 1987, the Women's Sports Foundation has presented an award in her honor to a woman who demonstrates Hyman's "dignity, spirit and commitment to excellence."

One of the winners of the Hyman Award was Mary Lou Retton, who won a gold medal in gymnastics at the 1984 Olympics. In 1988, Hyman was inducted into the Volleyball Hall of Fame in Holyoke, Massachusetts.

"Flo was our Babe Ruth," said U.S. Volleyball Association Executive Vice President William W. Baird.

If anything, volleyball has proven to be a haven for female athletes. On the college level it's almost exclusively a female sport. According to recent statistics, there are 911 colleges with women's teams and just 74 with men's volleyball programs.

Another standout player who has gained worldwide attention is 6' 3" Gabrielle "Gabby" Reece. Combining a stunning appearance and athletic ability, Reece became a contender on the beach circuit during the late 1990s and may have done more to promote the sport than anyone else at that time. Her model-like looks made her a strong attraction for media types

With her athletic good looks, Gabrielle Reece, shown attending the Espy Awards, was a spokeswoman for the game of volleyball.

looking for someone to talk about the sport. Magazines made her a frequent cover subject.

Reece was born on January 6, 1970, in California. Her mother, Terry Glenn, was from Long Island, and her father was from Trinidad. Her father died when she was just five years old. After her father's death, her mother sent Gabrielle to live with friends on Long Island and then later on St. Thomas, in the U.S. Virgin Islands. She lived there with friends until she was 15.

"I thought I would graduate from high school and work in a gift shop," Reece once told a reporter.

By the time Reece entered 11th grade, her mother moved her to St. Petersburg, Florida, to attend a private school. Like Flo Hyman, Reece came to the sport of volleyball a bit late, although her athleticism and height made up for any shortfall in early learning.

On the court, Reece stood apart from her teammates. She also stood out on the street, where her exotic beauty made heads turn. At about the same time she was taking up volleyball, she caught the eye of a modeling agent, who began landing Reece modeling jobs.

The money from modeling was so good that Reece considered dropping out of school. But she stayed and graduated, winning a volleyball scholarship to Florida State University (FSU).

At Florida State, Reece played two seasons while splitting time between a growing number of modeling jobs.

As a prominent volleyball player, Reece also found peace. "Volleyball anchored me at a time in my life when I needed it," she said. "It gave me a reason for being this big, big girl."

When Reece was a sophomore at Florida State, *Elle* magazine named her one of the five most beautiful women in the world. The draw of modeling—as well as the money that comes with being photographed—proved too strong for Reece. By her second year, she was splitting her time between Florida and New York, where she was a top model.

Often she had to turn down lucrative modeling jobs to play volleyball at Florida State, earning several All-Tournament awards. When she was a junior, the Dodge National Athletic Awards Committee named her the nation's Most Inspiring Collegiate Athlete.

After Florida State, a friend encouraged Reece to move to California and try doubles beach volleyball, where women play in teams of two. The doubles game was athletically more demanding than the game that she was used to, making her feel a bit out of place.

"I had no idea what I was doing," she once said. "I played for half a season with the Women's Professional Volleyball Association Tour and got my butt kicked."

Reece brought a new level of athleticism to the beach game. Typically, indoor players were considered the serious athletes, with the outdoor players not being as intense about the preparation. Reece changed that.

Preparation notwithstanding, Reece lasted a half-season before leaving the doubles series. Later, she was recruited to play in the Bud Light League, a newly formed four-on-four series, where she excelled, leading the league in blocks and kills in 1994, '95, and '96. In 1994 and 1995, she was voted the best offensive player. She also served as team captain for five seasons and was ranked fifth in the NCAA in career blocks. Her work in volleyball landed her a contract to promote Nike.

However, because of changes in the sport, Reece eventually had to return to the two-person game.

"I was really committed to 4s and resisting 2s for the longest time because I thought 4s would be my strength," she told the Ft. Lauderdale, Florida, *Sun-Sentinel* in 1998.

"But I have to be realistic. If I want to play beach volleyball, I have to play doubles. It's a pretty new game to me. I feel like a rookie. It's a little bit taking a chance for me but most of that comes from the fear of not representing myself really well. The biggest thing for me is I want to play volleyball first. I have made that commitment."

Representing herself and the game of volleyball were driving forces for Reece. Her looks drew attention, but her message was always clear: women can be attractive *and* good athletes.

In Gabrielle Reece's case, though, her looks helped land her television jobs, such as hosting a sports show for the cable music channel MTV.

"If I had my way, the balance I have worked to achieve in my life would be what stands out and not the fact that I am a good-looking woman who plays volleyball," she said. "I worked hard to get where I am."

Reece takes pride in being a role model for young women. "I see in their eyes that I'm living their dream," she said. "If I can inspire them to get there though hard work and discipline and enjoy their success, that's great."

She encourages young girls to play sports, rather than sit on the sidelines. "When you're just hanging out with chicks, you're deciding, 'Should we go to the mall or the movies?'" she told *USA Weekend*. "But on a team you set goals, you work together. If a teammate makes you angry, you can't say, 'I'm not hanging out with her anymore.' The best player may be the one who drives you nuts, but you understand her importance."

In addition to her performance on the beach, Reece considers what she wears important too. While some of her teammates and competitors wear athletic bikinis to play, she prefers a sports top and running tights. Doing so, she said, is part of helping break the stereotype of women's sports.

Holly McPeak hits the ball against France at the women's beach volleyball event at the 1996 summer Olympics in Atlanta.

Having Reece on the beach also helps bring fans and the media to the sport. In reality, beach volleyball would get little media attention on its own. But a star like Reece draws people's interest.

Partly because of Reece, fans have turned out to see such volleyball players as Mary Jo Peppler, Liz Masakayan, Lisa Arce, and Nancy Reno.

"That's life," says fellow beach volleyball standout Holly McPeak, who teamed with Reece in 1999. "If she can help promote our sport, that's fine with me. She can have a line 5,000 people long and if I don't have anyone asking for my autograph, it won't matter a bit as long as we win."

6

STARS OF TODAY AND TOMORROW

Thanks to players such as Karch Kiraly and Gabrielle Reece, the sport of volleyball, founded more than 100 years ago by William G. Morgan, is on solid ground.

The play of Kiraly and Reece, as well as their efforts to promote the game, helped lead others to seek out local volleyball teams and events in their areas.

But the game still lags way behind baseball, football, and hockey in popularity. Its growth years are usually built around the Olympics, when the Games generate wide media attention and television coverage.

Among the current beach volleyball stars are folks like Lisa Arce, a California native who was ranked 11th in the world during 1999. On the FIVB's international circuit, Arce had amassed more than $200,000 in prize winnings during her career.

Before turning to the professional ranks, Arce was a prominent player at the University of California. She left the school as its all-time leader in categories such as digs and attempts, two forms of hitting. She also helped lead the team to the NCAA Tournament in three seasons.

Another top female beach player is Annette Buckner Davis, a Long Beach, California, native who was ranked third overall by the FIVB in 1999. Davis helped lead UCLA to three NCAA championship appearances during her tenure

Holly McPeak, left, and Karch Kiraly are among the best in the world at their respective sports, men's and women's beach volleyball. By the end of the 20th century, beach volleyball had surpassed indoor volleyball in popularity.

there. A two-time all-American, she finished at UCLA among the highest scorers in school history. She was the PAC-10 player of the year in 1994.

A relative newcomer to the beach game is Jenny Johnson Jordan, a Tarzana, California, native. Like her competitors, Jordan was a superb player at UCLA, where she was named to the all-American team in 1994.

Jordan is the daughter of Rafer and Betsy Johnson, both of whom spent their lives around Olympic competition. Rafer Johnson won the gold medal in decathlon at the 1960 Olympics in Rome and claimed a silver medal at the 1956 Games in Melbourne, Australia.

Leading men's beach players include Dain Blanton, Ian Clark, Sinjin Smith, and Kevin Wong.

The U.S.'s Sinjin Smith dives for the ball during the men's Olympic beach volleyball match against Portugal at the Centennial Olympic Games in Atlanta.

Blanton, from Laguna Beach, California, was an all-American player at Pepperdine University, helping lead the team to an NCAA championship in 1992. In 1999, he was ranked number 22 in the FIVB standings and had earned $63,550 in prize money from just 18 pro events in his career.

Blanton's teammate on the 1992 Pepperdine championship team was Ian Clark, who was born in Boulder, Colorado. Clark joined the professional circuit in 1994 and had his best year on the Association of Professionals Tour in 1997, when he placed in the top five in seven tournaments. In 14 FIVB events in his career, Clark earned $66,500 in prize money. Besides volleyball, Clark spent some time as a child actor on the television show *CHiPs*.

Sinjin Smith, one of the veterans of the professional circuit, is the all-time winningest player on the AVP tour, with 139 career titles. He is one of the pioneers of the international game, playing in 73 events dating back to 1987.

Before going pro, Smith was an all-American at UCLA, playing on two National Championship teams there. He was the first volleyball player inducted into the school's sports hall of fame. Playing in 82 FIVB events, Smith has earned more than $384,813 in prize money. He's been part of the winning team on 10 occasions.

Kevin Wong is one of the rising stars of the beach game; 1999 was his third year on the pro circuit. A native of Honolulu, Hawaii, Wong was a member of two National Championship teams at UCLA, earning all-American honors twice. In three seasons, Wong earned $62,200

Brigham Young's Ryan Millar, right, spikes the ball against Penn State's Brad Miller during the first game of their May 6, 1999, NCAA Volleyball Championship semifinals match.

in prize money on the FIVB tour, with a third place finish in 1999 his best-ever finish.

As of 1999, the U.S. National team was populated with seasoned players who were all stars in their own right before joining the squad that would represent the country in international competition.

Among the women's players, Demetria Sance, a San Antonio Native, has been one of only eight players to have ever earned all-American honors in four collegiate seasons. Sance also performed well at the 2000 Nike Americas' Volleyball Challenge, where she was starting left-side hitter.

Stacy Sykora, a Burleson, Texas, native, saw her first international action in Australia during the 1999 season. She was the primary passer and defensive player on the U.S. team that earned a bronze medal at the Pan American Games.

Mickisha Hurley hails from Miami, Florida, and, along with Stacy Sykora, helped the U.S. women's team earn the bronze medal at the Pan American Games. Hurley was starting middle blocker at the Nike Americas' Volleyball Challenge held in January of 2000, where the U.S. women's National team defeated Canada to qualify for the 2000 Olympics in Sydney, Australia.

Danielle Scott, from Baton Rouge, Louisiana, also played on the bronze medal-winning team at the 1999 Pan American Games. A three-time American Volleyball Association first-team, all-American, Scott saw action in the final two Olympic matches of 1996.

Macare Desilets racked up a team high of 13 kills against Cuba at the 1999 World Cup. The 6' 2" outside hitter played for the University of Washington, where she holds records for career blocks-solo, block assists, and total blocks.

Terri Demaitis, a 6' 2" middle blocker from Downer's Grove, Illinois, recorded nine kills, five blocks, and a .400 hitting percentage at the 2000 Nike Americas' Volleyball Challenge. At Penn State, Demaitis led her team to Big Ten Conference titles and is the only player in Big Ten history to record more than 1,500 kills, 1,000 digs, and 600 blocks.

Among the men leading the way for the indoor teams is 6' 5" Greg Romano, a Racine,

Wisconsin, native who studied at Ball State, where he was an all-American in 1995.

Another Ball State star was Phil Eatherton, from Glencoe, Missouri, who ended his career at Ball State as the all-time leader in blocks and block assists. He helped the team reach the NCAA finals in 1977.

Middle blocker Ryan Millar hails from Palmdale, California, and attended Brigham Young University, where he was one of only five players to earn the American Volleyball Coaches Association first-team all-American honors three times. Millar helped the men's team qualify for the 2000 Sydney Olympics with 25 kills, four blocks, and three aces at the 2000 Continental Cup.

Jeff Nygaard, from Madison, Wisconsin, attended UCLA and helped lead the team to two National Championships. He joined the National team in 1995, where he made an immediate impact.

At 6' 10" Chris Harger is the tallest player on the U.S. men's 2000 volleyball team. A middle blocker who hails from Long Beach, California, Harger played for the University of California at Irvine, where he holds the record for the most career blocks with 372 assists and 451 total blocks.

Mike Lambert of Kaneohe, Hawaii, led the men's National team with 12 kills and a .563 hitting percentage in its Olympic-qualifying win over Canada at the 2000 Continental Cup. At Stanford University, Lambert was ranked number two in kills and aces and third in blocks.

These are just a few of the players who will be leading the sport in the new millennium. And, in reality, there are others out there right now, hitting a ball over a net in a backyard or in a gymnasium, who down the road will be representing the United States on the volley-ball court.

It's doubtful that William G. Morgan could have ever imagined his sport of Mintonette getting as big as it is today.

CHRONOLOGY

1895	William G. Morgan invents the game of Mintonette.
1896	Mintonette is renamed Volley ball (and is later lowercased and made one word).
1900	A special ball is designed for volleyball; Canada becomes the first country outside of the United States to adopt the sport.
1906	Soldiers introduce volleyball to Cuba.
1922	The first YMCA National Championships are held in Brooklyn, N.Y.; players on 27 teams representing 11 states take part in the tournament.
1928	The U.S. Volleyball Association is created as the sport's official national governing body.
1930	The first two-man beach volleyball game is played in California.
1947	The Federation Internationale de Volley Ball (FIVB) is formed to oversee the sport around the globe; the first official two-man beach volleyball tournament is held at State Beach in California.
1948	The first World Championships are held in Prague, Czechoslovakia.
1964	Men's and women's volleyball are introduced as official Olympic sports.
1965	The California Beach Volleyball Association is founded to promote tournaments.
1974	The first commercially sponsored beach volleyball tournament takes place in San Diego, California.
1983	The Association of Volleyball Professionals (AVP) is formed.
1984	The U.S. Men's team wins its first-ever Olympic gold medal in Los Angeles.
1988	The U.S. Men's team wins its second Olympic gold medal in Seoul, South Korea.
1995	The 100th birthday of volleyball is celebrated around the world.
1996	Two-person beach volleyball is added to the Olympics in Atlanta, Georgia; the U.S. men's team wins the gold medal.
1999	The U.S. women's team wins a bronze medal at the Pan American Games.
2000	The U.S. women's team defeats Canada at the Nike America's Volleyball Challenge to qualify for the 2000 Olympics in Sydney, Australia; the U.S. men's team qualifies at the Continental Cup for the 2000 Olympics.

GLOSSARY

ACE
A serve that scores a point without an opposing player touching the ball.

BLOCK
Occurs when a player jumping in the air and using his or her hands prevents the ball from passing over the net.

COURT
The area in which a volleyball game is played.

DIG
A move whereby a player hits a ball below waist-height.

KILL
A shot that is impossible for an opponent to return.

MATCH
A predetermined number of games combined represent one match. Typically, indoor matches are decided in a best-of-three contest.

NET BALL
A ball that touches the net.

POINT
A team that is serving scores a point when the ball hits the court on the opponent's side of the net.

RALLY
The time when the ball is in play after being served.

ROTATION
When a team gets the ball back to serve, players rotate one position clockwise.

SET

A high pass from one player to another.

SPIKE

A rapid hit—usually after the ball has been "set" by another player—that sends the ball hard to the court.

VOLLEY

A series of plays in which the ball is hit back and forth between teams.

FURTHER READING

Gaines, Ann Graham. *Sports and Athletics*. Philadelphia: Chelsea House Publishers, 1999.

Howard, Robert E. *An Understanding of the Fundamental Techniques of Volleyball*. Needham Heights, Massachusetts: Allyn and Bacon, 1995.

Kiraly, Karch, and Byron Shewman. *Beach Volleyball*. Champaign, Illinois: Human Kinetics Books, 1999.

Martin, Peggy. *101 Volleyball Drills*. Champaign, Illinois: Coaches Choice, 1999.

Reece, Gabrielle, and Karen Karbo. *Big Girl in the Middle*. New York: Crown, 1997.

WEBSITES

www.volleyball.org
Volleyball World Wide

www.usavolleyball.org
USA Volleyball

INDEX

PICTURE CREDITS Associated Press/WWP: pp. 2, 6, 8, 10, 24, 27, 30, 35, 37, 40, 44, 49, 50, 52, 54, 58; Jeffrey Eisenberg: p. 46; National Archives: p. 12, 18, 28; Volleyball Hall of Fame: pp. 14, 16, 20, 32, 33, 42.

RICHARD HUFF is an award-winning author. His previous books include *Behind The Wall: A Season on the NASCAR Circuit*, *The Insider's Guide to Stock Car Racing*, *The Making of a Race Car*, *The Jarretts*, *Formula One Racing,* and *Demolition Derby*. He is a staff writer and motorsports columnist for the *New York Daily News*. His work has appeared in such national publications as *Circle Track*, *Inside NASCAR*, *Stock Car Racing Magazine*, *The Washington Journalism Review*, *Video Review,* and *NASCAR Magazine*. He lives in New Jersey with his wife, Michelle, son, Ryan, and daughter, Paige.

ACKNOWLEDGMENTS: Special thanks to Michelle, Ryan, and Paige for all of their support.